GW01401344

Original title:
Pure Joy

Author: Thor Castlebury
ISBN HARDBACK: 978-9916-88-210-8
ISBN PAPERBACK: 978-9916-88-211-5

Awakening Elation

In morning's light, dreams arise,
The heart expands, the spirit flies.
A whisper soft, a gentle breeze,
Elation blooms beneath the trees.

With every step, the world aglow,
Joy dances lightly, sweet and slow.
Each moment sparkles, time unfolds,
Awakening warmth, a tale retold.

Boundless Wonder

In fields of green, where visions play,
Curious minds chase night and day.
Each leaf a puzzle, a tale unspun,
Boundless wonder has just begun.

Stars whisper secrets, the moon draws near,
Magic surrounds, dissolving all fear.
In every heartbeat, in every glance,
Life is a canvas, an endless chance.

Sunshine Serenade

Golden rays through branches weave,
A serenade that makes me believe.
Warmth wraps around, dispels the cold,
Each note a story, a life retold.

Laughter echoes in clear blue skies,
Joy paints the world before our eyes.
In this embrace, our hearts ignite,
Sunshine's melody, pure and bright.

Kaleidoscope of Happiness

Colors swirl in joyous dance,
A kaleidoscope, a fleeting chance.
Every shade tells a tale of glee,
Moments of bliss, wild and free.

Through laughter and love, life spins around,
In this vibrant world, peace is found.
Hearts intertwine, forever to be,
A tapestry woven of you and me.

Heartfelt Whirls

In the quiet of the night,
Whispers dance in gentle light.
Hearts entwined, a soft embrace,
Lost in love's enchanted space.

Stars above begin to sway,
Guiding dreams that drift away.
Moments cherished, time stands still,
In the warmth of pure goodwill.

Through the shadows, bright and bold,
Every story yet untold.
Timeless feelings start to shine,
In the bliss where hearts align.

Enchanted Gatherings

Underneath the ancient tree,
Laughter flows, so wild and free.
Friends and family gather near,
Creating bonds that feel so dear.

In the circle, stories blend,
Golden moments, time to spend.
Unified by love's sweet call,
Together we shall rise, not fall.

With the sunset painting skies,
Hope and joy before our eyes.
Each embrace a treasure found,
In the magic that surrounds.

Jubilant Steps

With each step, we find a way,
To embrace the bright new day.
Hearts leap high, spirits soar,
In the rhythm, we explore.

Path of joy beneath our feet,
Every heartbeat feels the beat.
Dancing in the morning light,
Chasing shadows out of sight.

Through the valleys, over hills,
Life unfolds with vibrant thrills.
In the music, we shall trust,
Jubilant steps, arise we must.

The Joyful Tapestry

Threads of laughter, colors bright,
Woven into day and night.
Stories told in vibrant hue,
Crafting life with joys anew.

Every moment, every thread,
Lays the path we choose to tread.
In this tapestry we weave,
Layers of love we all believe.

From each heart, a piece unfolds,
Shining brightly, never cold.
In this dance of dreams and fate,
We create a life ornate.

Nurturing Merriment

In a garden of laughter, we bloom bright,
Every moment a treasure, pure delight.
Joyful whispers dance in the air,
Together in harmony, free of care.

Through playful games and smiles we share,
Friendship's embrace is ever so rare.
With hearts wide open, we sing our song,
In this world of bliss, we all belong.

Celestial Joyride

Stars twinkle down in the velvet night,
Guiding our dreams with a gentle light.
We ride through the cosmos, hand in hand,
In the galaxy's arms, we take our stand.

Comets streak by, painting trails so bright,
In the sky's vast canvas, we find our flight.
With laughter and wonder, we soar so high,
In the whispers of starlight, we'll never die.

Sunshine Between Raindrops

A storm may come, but we still find cheer,
For after the rain, the sun draws near.
With drops of silver, the world will gleam,
In puddles of joy, we chase our dream.

The rainbow arches, a promise renewed,
In every setback, hope is imbued.
With laughter and light amidst the gray,
We dance through the storm, come what may.

Lively Heartbeats

With every pulse, a rhythm unfolds,
In the dance of life, our story's told.
We move to the beat of joy so sweet,
In the vibrant flow, our spirits meet.

Together we sway, like trees in the breeze,
Each heartbeat a note, a promise to seize.
In the symphony of existence, we play,
A chorus of love, brightening the day.

Golden Glimmers

In the dawn's embrace, light takes flight,
Whispers of warmth in soft morning light.
Every dewdrop shines, a world anew,
Promises linger in each fading hue.

Golden rays dance on leaves of green,
Nature's ballet, a tranquil scene.
Moments captured, so fleeting and sweet,
A tapestry woven where dreams and reality meet.

Underneath skies painted with gold,
Stories of love and courage unfold.
The heart beats softly, a rhythmic call,
In golden glimmers, we find it all.

The Pulse of Elation

Dancing shadows in the evening air,
Laughter and joy, a melody rare.
The world around sparkles with grace,
Every heartbeat quickens this vibrant space.

In the rhythm of life, we find our place,
Moments of bliss, a shimmering chase.
With eyes wide open, we strive to feel,
The pulse of elation, a joy that's real.

Through the labyrinth of dreams we roam,
Finding our way, we're never alone.
In every smile and every embrace,
The pulse of elation, a sacred space.

A Dance Beyond Words

Under moonlit skies, feet find their way,
In silent rhythms, we drift and sway.
No need for language, just hearts that know,
In the dance beyond words, our spirits flow.

Glimmers of laughter, shadows entwine,
A timeless journey, your hand in mine.
Every twirl whispers what hearts would say,
In this magic, we willingly stay.

With each gentle turn, stories unfold,
A universe written in motions bold.
Lost in the moment, we twirl and twine,
A dance beyond words, infinitely divine.

The Splendor of Now

In the stillness of time, beauty resides,
Moments unwrapped, where joy abides.
A sunset's glow, the touch of a breeze,
In the splendor of now, the soul finds ease.

Every heartbeat echoes, a tender song,
Reminding us gently where we belong.
In laughter and silence, life's light is shown,
In the splendor of now, we're never alone.

With open hearts, we embrace each day,
Finding our bliss in the simplest way.
As time dances softly, let go of the how,
And breathe in the beauty, the splendor of now.

Unfurling Smiles

In the dawn's gentle light,
Joy begins to bloom,
Each smile a fragrant flower,
Chasing away the gloom.

Laughter dances on air,
Warmth in every glance,
Hearts open wide and free,
In this cheerful dance.

With every shared moment,
Bonds are woven tight,
Unfurling like petals,
In the morning's light.

Radiant Heartbeats

With every thump and pulse,
Life's rhythm plays on,
A melody of joy,
Like a sweet, gentle song.

In the quiet of night,
Stars twinkle above,
Whispers of heartbeats,
Echoes of our love.

Together we sway,
In the soft moon's glow,
Each heartbeat a promise,
In the night's gentle flow.

A Symphony of Cheer

Each laugh a vibrant note,
In the air they soar,
Creating a symphony,
We can't help but adore.

Friendship strums the chords,
Every heartbeat's tune,
Melodies of happiness,
Under the bright moon.

Join hands in the rhythm,
Dance free with delight,
In this joyful concert,
Our spirits take flight.

Skylark Serenade

Above the lush green fields,
Skylarks take their flight,
Singing songs of freedom,
In the morning light.

With wings spread wide they soar,
Their music fills the air,
A serenade of hope,
For all who stop and stare.

Nature hums along too,
In this grand ballet,
The skylarks' sweet voices,
Guide us through the day.

Sunlit Laughter

In the morning light, we play,
Joyful echoes fill the day.
Chasing shadows, hearts take flight,
Together we shine, oh so bright.

With a smile, the world does bloom,
Every moment, laughter's tune.
Hands entwined, a dance we weave,
In this magic, we believe.

Dancing on Clouds

Floating high where dreams embrace,
We glide through time, a gentle pace.
With each twirl, the sky does sing,
Lost in joy, our spirits spring.

Colors swirl in a blissful haze,
In this moment, we are amazed.
Step by step, we lose all fear,
Together, love is all we hear.

Whispers of Delight

Softly spoken words of cheer,
Wrap around us, ever near.
In this hush, love gently grows,
In every heartbeat, mystery flows.

Golden glimmers in the night,
Guiding us to purest light.
With each laughter, bonds unfold,
Tales of treasures yet untold.

The Color of Happiness

Brushstrokes of joy paint the sky,
With every color, we learn to fly.
In vibrant hues, we find our way,
Crafting memories day by day.

A spectrum bright, love intertwines,
In the laughter, the world aligns.
With hearts aglow, we dance anew,
In the warmth of smiles, dreams come true.

Dancing in the Rain

Pitter patter on the ground,
Feet embrace the muddy sound,
Twirling under cloudy skies,
Laughter echoes, spirit flies.

Raindrops fall like silver beads,
Nature's rhythm, heart it feeds,
Splashing puddles, joy alight,
Dancing shadows, pure delight.

Whirling dresses, twinkling eyes,
Every heartbeat, pure surprise,
Wind and rain, a glorious dance,
In this moment, take a chance.

Celebrate the stormy night,
In the chaos, find your light,
Dancing freely, no refrain,
Life's a song, we sing in rain.

Heartstrings Unbound

In the quiet, whispers flow,
Hidden feelings start to grow,
Gentle touches, fingers weave,
Stories shared, we both believe.

Memories linger, sweet and warm,
Through the silence, hearts can swarm,
Every glance a precious thread,
In this dance, our souls are fed.

Entwined paths that twist and turn,
Through the fire, passions burn,
With each heartbeat, we expand,
In this realm, our spirits stand.

Boundless love, a timeless song,
Together, where we all belong,
Ties that link and never fray,
Heartstrings unbound, come what may.

Joyful Reverie

In the morning, sun awakes,
Softly painted, light it makes,
Golden beams through window pane,
Whispers of a world unstained.

Children laughing, carefree play,
Chasing sunlight, bright bouquet,
Butterflies in vibrant flight,
Dance of colors, pure delight.

Moments cherished, fleeting fast,
Hold them close, forever last,
Daydreams float on gentle breeze,
Joyful hearts sing melodies.

In our reverie, we find,
Beauty that can soothe the mind,
Life's a canvas, bright and free,
In this joy, we find our glee.

Blossoms of Delight

In the garden, colors bloom,
Fragrant petals chase the gloom,
Nature's laughter fills the air,
Joy in blossoms everywhere.

Dew drops glisten in the morn,
With each sunbeam, hope is born,
Little creatures dance and play,
Life awakens in its sway.

Underneath the azure sky,
Butterflies and birds drift by,
Chasing dreams on soft spring breeze,
Whispered secrets through the trees.

Every flower tells a tale,
Of the winds and gentle hail,
In this bounty, hearts take flight,
Finding peace in sheer delight.

Sparkling Moments

In the morning light, we rise anew,
With laughter bright, and skies so blue.
Each tiny spark, a joyful gleam,
In fleeting time, we chase the dream.

Whispers of joy dance in the air,
Memories twinkling, beyond compare.
We gather each fragment, hold it tight,
In sparkling moments, pure delight.

The sunset glows, a canvas fire,
Colors collide, hearts lift higher.
With friends beside, we share the glow,
In sparkling moments, love will flow.

As starlit nights begin to call,
We cherish each memory, one and all.
In every heartbeat, the magic stays,
In sparkling moments, forever plays.

Radiant Souls

Beneath the sun, we shine so bright,
In gentle hearts, our hopes take flight.
With every smile, a spark ignites,
Radiant souls, in joyful lights.

Through every storm, we stand as one,
Together we rise, till the day is done.
In laughter's embrace, we find our way,
Radiant souls, come what may.

When shadows fall, we'll light the night,
With warmth that echoes, pure and right.
In each sweet moment, love unfolds,
Radiant souls, more precious than gold.

In softest whispers, connections grow,
A tapestry woven, hearts aglow.
Through every trial, we find our roles,
In harmony's dance, radiant souls.

The Color of Bliss

A splash of joy, in every hue,
The color of bliss, painted anew.
With vivid dreams, we find our song,
In life's bright palette, we all belong.

The golden glow of a sunny morn,
In laughter shared, our hearts are born.
With every sunrise, hope takes flight,
The color of bliss, in sheer delight.

Through fields of green, our spirits play,
In nature's embrace, we find our way.
Every moment cherished, a brush of grace,
The color of bliss, in time and space.

When twilight whispers, the stars align,
In quiet beauty, our souls entwine.
With every heartbeat, love we kiss,
In every shade, the color of bliss.

Echoes of Happiness

In the laughter shared, we hear the sound,
Echoes of happiness, all around.
With every joy, a melody rings,
In the heart's embrace, love gently sings.

Through joyful moments, time shall flow,
In the rhythm of life, our spirits glow.
Each memory cherished, forever stays,
Echoes of happiness, in countless ways.

As seasons change, we'll hold them tight,
In the warmth of love, all feels right.
Through trials faced, we stand as one,
Echoes of happiness, never done.

With every heartbeat, we sing along,
A symphony crafted, a timeless song.
In every glance, a spark ignites,
Echoes of happiness, pure delights.

Golden Sunlit Paths

Golden rays warm the earth,
Flowers dance, a moment of mirth.
Whispers of breezes soft and light,
Walk with me into the bright.

Fields of dreams stretch far and wide,
Nature's canvas, a gentle guide.
Footprints shared in sweet embrace,
As we wander, time's a grace.

Branches sway, a lullaby's tune,
Beneath the watchful afternoon moon.
Every path leads to new sights,
Bathed in the warmth of golden lights.

Together we'll chase the day,
On sunlit paths, we find our way.
With hearts aglow, we will roam,
In this paradise, we feel at home.

Blossoming Laughter

In gardens bright, laughter blooms,
Joyful echoes dispel all glooms.
Children play, their giggles ring,
Happiness is what they bring.

Every petal tells a tale,
A symphony of colors prevail.
With smiles like sunshine in spring,
In their joy, our spirits take wing.

Moments shared in pure delight,
Filling hearts with warmth so bright.
As blossoms sway with playful dance,
Laughter weaves a sweet romance.

Together we find our song,
In each heartbeat, we belong.
With hands held tight, we cannot fall,
Our laughter blooms, embracing all.

Floating on a Cloud

Soft and white, the clouds above,
Carry dreams on wings of love.
Floating high, we leave the ground,
In this realm, peace knows no bound.

Gentle whispers in the air,
Worries fade; we shed our care.
Drifting free in azure skies,
Finding joy where the heart lies.

Sunset paints the world below,
In hues of gold, a radiant glow.
With each breath, we float anew,
On a cloud of dreams, just me and you.

Time stands still in this embrace,
Together we explore this space.
With hearts as light as feathered wings,
We dance where the freedom sings.

Melodies of Celebration

Underneath a starry dome,
Music calls us to our home.
Rhythms pulse through every heart,
Join the dance, let joy impart.

Voices lifted to the night,
Singing songs that feel so right.
In the circle, laughter flows,
As the warmth of friendship grows.

Candles flicker, bright and clear,
Wishes whispered, dreams sincere.
In this moment, time stands still,
With every note, our spirits thrill.

Hand in hand, we celebrate,
Every heartbeat, love's sweet fate.
Together we'll create the sound,
In these melodies, joy is found.

Laughter in the Breeze

Laughter dances in the air,
Whispering secrets everywhere.
Sunlight twinkling on the grass,
Joyful moments come to pass.

Children playing, voices bright,
Kites are soaring, pure delight.
Colors blending in the sky,
Echoes of happiness nearby.

Waves of giggles ride the gust,
In the warmth, we place our trust.
Nature sings a lullaby,
With every chuckle, spirits fly.

So let us bask in this embrace,
In the laughter, find our place.
For in the breeze, our hearts will sing,
And celebrate the joy we bring.

.

Hues of Exuberance

A canvas painted, bold and bright,
Colors bursting, pure delight.
Yellows, reds, and shades of green,
In this palette, life is seen.

Brushstrokes dance with every hue,
A vibrant world, forever new.
Nature's art, a grand display,
Filled with laughter, come what may.

Each flower blooms with a smile,
Reflecting joy, if just a while.
In every corner, zest abounds,
Exuberance in leaps and bounds.

Let the colors swirl and play,
In our hearts, they light the way.
A celebration, life defined,
In these hues, true peace we find.

Unfurling Radiance

Morning light begins to spill,
Illuminating every hill.
Petals open, greet the sun,
A new day's promise has begun.

Glimmers dance on leaves of jade,
Nature's beauty, unafraid.
Every shadow meets the light,
In this moment, hearts take flight.

Warmth surrounds us, softly glows,
In this radiance, laughter flows.
Hope like flowers, blooms anew,
Unfurling dreams in every view.

Together, let our spirits rise,
In the glow of painted skies.
For in this warmth, we find our way,
To brighter tomorrows, come what may.

Canvas of Smiles

A canvas bright, where joy resides,
Every smile, a wave that glides.
Colors splashed with tender care,
In this art, the world to share.

Brush of kindness strokes the day,
Painting hopes in vibrant array.
Every laugh, a touch of grace,
Bringing light to every face.

In this gallery, hearts unite,
Finding warmth in shared delight.
With every moment, joy unspools,
As life unfolds, we paint the rules.

So let us gather, hearts in sync,
Crafting dreams with every ink.
On this canvas, let love stream,
A masterpiece of every dream.

Fields of Delight

In the meadow where the flowers sway,
Sunshine dances, brightening the day.
A gentle breeze whispers through the grass,
Each moment cherished, never to pass.

Butterflies flutter, a colorful flight,
Beneath the blue sky, everything feels right.
Joy springs forth in each bloom so bold,
Nature's canvas, a beauty to behold.

The laughter of children, carefree and loud,
Echoes of happiness, a gathering crowd.
In fields of delight, where dreams intertwine,
Time stands still, like a sweet glass of wine.

Gentle Giggles

In the quiet corners of a sunny space,
Giggles arise, painting smiles on each face.
The warmth of laughter, a soothing sound,
In this gentle moment, joy is found.

Tickling hands and soft, playful glee,
Children at play, wild and carefree.
A game of chase, weaving in and out,
Every chuckle echoes, no hint of doubt.

As shadows grow longer, the laughter will fade,
But hints of the giggles in hearts will be laid.
These fleeting joys, like petals in flight,
Bring warmth to our souls, morning and night.

Embrace the Present

Here and now, this moment is ours,
Time stands still, beneath twinkling stars.
Inhale the beauty, let worries drift,
Each heartbeat a treasure, a precious gift.

Forget the past, the future's a dream,
Find joy in the river, the sun's gentle beam.
Let each whisper of wind tell you to stay,
Embrace the present, come what may.

Savor the taste of the morning dew,
Feel the warmth of the sun breaking through.
In the dance of life, let moments be right,
Hold close the magic, the day and the night.

Retreat into Happiness

Find a quiet spot, where peace can dwell,
A sanctuary built like a wishing well.
In stillness, discover what makes you whole,
Retreat into happiness, nourish your soul.

With a book in hand, or a pen and some dreams,
Let your thoughts flow like gentle streams.
Close your eyes, feel the world fade away,
In this cozy nook, it's okay to stay.

Nature's embrace, a soft lullaby,
Under branches that sway with the sky.
Here in the stillness, let worries release,
Retreat into happiness, find your sweet peace.

Fields of Elation

In morning's glow, the flowers bloom,
Bright colors dance, dispelling gloom.
With every breeze, the moments sing,
In fields of joy, our hearts take wing.

The sun bestows its golden grace,
As laughter echoes, we find our place.
Each step we take, the joy we weave,
In fields of elation, we believe.

The gentle rustle of the grass,
In nature's arms, our worries pass.
With friends beside, we share the day,
In fields of gold, we'll laugh and play.

A canvas painted, pure delight,
Where dreams are born and spirits light.
Together here, we dance and sway,
In fields of elation, come what may.

Bubbles of Laughter

In gardens bright, the bubbles rise,
Reflecting joy beneath the skies.
With every pop, a giggle flows,
In innocence, true happiness grows.

They twirl and spin in playful flight,
A dance of warmth, in purest light.
Each laughter shared, a glowing trace,
Bubbles of joy, we can't replace.

As children chase, the world feels free,
In every smile, we find the key.
To cherish moments, fleeting fast,
In bubbles of laughter, we are cast.

So let us play, with hearts so true,
In every bubble, love shines through.
A treasure shared, forever lasts,
In bubbles of laughter, remembrances amassed.

Infinite Smiles

Across the dawn, where sunlight spills,
Warmth blankets all, the heart it fills.
In every glance, a spark ignites,
With infinite smiles, the world excites.

Two friends entwined in joyful play,
A bond that time cannot betray.
With every chuckle, spirits rise,
In infinite smiles, we touch the skies.

Each moment shared, a fleeting chance,
Like whispered tales in a timeless dance.
Through trials faced, we find the style,
Together living with infinite smiles.

So here we stand, through thick and thin,
In every laughter, we always win.
Embrace the light, stay close awhile,
For life is brighter with infinite smiles.

Sweet Whispers of Life

In quiet moments, secrets dwell,
Between the leaves, the stories swell.
A gentle breeze, a soft reply,
Sweet whispers of life, beneath the sky.

Each heartbeat sings, a tender tune,
As twilight falls, beneath the moon.
In shared silence, our souls unite,
Sweet whispers of life, pure and right.

The stars above, they softly gleam,
Each twinkle holds a hidden dream.
In every glance, our hearts converse,
Sweet whispers of life, forever immersed.

So pause awhile, in nature's grace,
Let love's embrace fill up the space.
In simple joy, our spirits thrive,
With sweet whispers of life, we're alive.

The Magic of Togetherness

In the heart where laughter grows,
Hand in hand, through highs and lows.
Moments shared, a cherished art,
Binding souls, never apart.

Together we climb the hills,
Filling dreams with joyful thrills.
Every whisper, every glance,
Crafting our own sweet romance.

Enchanted Whimsy

In a world where dreams take flight,
Colors dance in pure delight.
Whimsical creatures roam the glade,
Magic thrives in joyous parade.

Bubbles float on gentle air,
Twinkling stars hang everywhere.
With each giggle, joy expands,
Filling life with merry bands.

Whispers of Laughter

In twilight's glow, the laughter sings,
Joyful echoes on angel's wings.
Soft whispers brush against the night,
Illuminating hearts so bright.

Memories twirl in playful cheer,
Bringing warmth to those held dear.
Echoes linger, sweet and clear,
In every moment, love draws near.

Glistening Sunbeams

Golden rays through branches weave,
Nature's canvas, pure reprieve.
Every shimmer, a soft embrace,
Lighting up the hidden space.

With each dawn, new hopes arise,
Painting warmth across the skies.
Life awakens with vibrant song,
In sunbeams, where hearts belong.

Sprinkles of Sunshine

Sunlight dances on the floor,
Jubilant whispers from the door.
Petals glisten, colors bright,
A soft embrace, pure delight.

Morning glows with warmth anew,
Each delight feels like a dew.
Joyful laughter fills the air,
As nature sparkles everywhere.

Radiant beams through leafy trees,
Kissing blooms with playful ease.
Every corner, every nook,
A world of wonder, take a look!

Sprinkles of sunshine, a gentle kiss,
In every moment, find your bliss.
Let the rays all drift and sway,
As happiness finds its way.

Embrace of Elation

In the arms of laughter's tune,
Hearts unite beneath the moon.
Waves of joy, like ocean's flow,
Together, in our spirits glow.

Every smile a cherished spark,
Guiding us through the endless dark.
Moments shared, both near and far,
We find our light, our guiding star.

Whispers wrapped in warm embrace,
In a world that feels like grace.
Rays of hope in twilight's beam,
Chasing shadows, living the dream.

In the dance of joy we spin,
With every breath, the heart can win.
Together, in elation's sway,
Finding bliss in every day.

The Luminous Path

Beneath the stars, a trail unfolds,
Guiding us where silence holds.
Each step bright with dreams to weave,
In this glow, we dare believe.

Lanterns flicker, tales to tell,
Wanderers in the night do dwell.
With every heartbeat, light ignites,
Illuminating endless nights.

Through the shadows, bold we stride,
Hand in hand, a joyful ride.
In the glow of hope we bask,
Finding strength in every task.

The luminous path, ours to share,
Guiding us with gentle care.
Through the journey, hearts in sync,
On this trail, we paint and think.

Heartstrings Strumming

In the rhythm of a gentle breeze,
Heartstrings hum, they twist and tease.
Melodies of love arise,
Echoes soft as starlit skies.

Every note, a story spun,
In each pulse, our lives are one.
Together, singing life's sweet song,
Finding where we all belong.

Whispers of the past entwined,
In this tapestry, we're blind.
Yet, with every strum and beat,
We ignite love, oh so sweet.

Heartstrings strumming, feel the sound,
In this harmony, we're found.
Let the music guide the way,
In our hearts, we'll dance and play.

Radiance in Reflection

In the mirror's gaze, a light,
Whispers dance, soft and bright.
Moments freeze, time stands still,
Heartbeats echo, a calming thrill.

Shadows play in gentle hues,
Every glance, a thoughtful muse.
Illuminated paths unfold,
Stories of the heart retold.

Crimson dawn, fading night,
Stars emerge in silent flight.
Reflections glow, dreams ignite,
A journey found in pure delight.

In each shimmer, truth laid bare,
Echoes linger in the air.
Through the glass, the world aligns,
Radiance found in heart's designs.

Dreamy Surrender

Underneath the velvet sky,
Whispers of the night float by.
Eyes are closed, breath is deep,
In this moment, secrets keep.

Stars above begin to twirl,
In the stillness, dreams unfurl.
Time, a river, softly flows,
Into the night, our spirit grows.

Clouds like pillows, drifting slow,
In the dark, where thoughts can glow.
Every sigh a gentle plea,
Lost in the depths of reverie.

As the dawn begins to creep,
In the twilight, love will seep.
Dreams will linger, hearts will blend,
In this surrender, we transcend.

The Serene Ecstasy

Gentle breeze through whispering trees,
Nature's sigh sings sweet relief.
In the calm, the heart finds ease,
Wrapped in love, beyond belief.

Rippling streams, the laughter flows,
Each moment bright, pure ecstasy.
Footsteps dance on petals' prose,
In the balance, we are free.

Sunlit meadows, endless spreads,
Where serenity finds its home.
In the stillness, joy embeds,
Lost in beauty's soft, sweet dome.

Here we linger, souls entwined,
In the silence, peace we find.
Serene faces, laughter shared,
In this ecstasy, life is bared.

A Symphony of Grins

In the hall of laughter's glow,
Every smile begins to flow.
Notes of joy in every heart,
Here, together, never part.

Rhythms dance in playful ways,
Crescendo in the sunlit rays.
Twirling dreams with every spin,
Life's a tune time can't rescind.

Echoes of our shared delight,
Chasing shadows, holding tight.
In this song, we find our place,
A symphony of endless grace.

Through the laughter, through the cheer,
In this moment, all is clear.
With each grin, our hearts do blend,
In this music, love transcends.

A Daydream in Bloom

In a garden bright, colors gleam,
Petals dance lightly, a soft, sweet dream.
Whispers of fragrance, in warm, gentle air,
Nature's embrace, a moment so rare.

Sunlight cascades on the dewy green,
Each leaf a treasure, a vibrant sheen.
Time drifts slowly, lost in this space,
In a daydream warm, we find our place.

Clouds lazily float, painting the sky,
Birds sing their songs as they gracefully fly.
Every heartbeat syncs with the rustling leaves,
In this bloom of stillness, the spirit believes.

Holding this magic, we linger and sigh,
In a world suspended, where moments comply.
Here, the heart thrives on the sweet perfume,
Life's sweetest chapter, a daydream in bloom.

Chasing Butterflies

Dancing through gardens, with laughter and glee,
Chasing the whispers, of each fluttered plea.
Colors in motion, as they take to the air,
Each fleeting moment, a treasure so rare.

With every step taken, joy fills the ground,
Their delicate wings, softly spinning around.
In fields of wildflowers, we skip and we sway,
Chasing the butterflies, lost in the play.

Time holds its breath, as they flit and they glide,
Two souls intertwined, with nature as guide.
In the chase of the fleeting, we find our delight,
A journey of wonder, painted in light.

So let us remember, this magical game,
Chasing the butterflies, hearts never the same.
In the canvas of nature, our spirits take flight,
Together we dance, beneath the soft light.

The Glittering Moment

In the hush of twilight, stars begin to shine,
Moments like diamonds, in a world so divine.
Whispers of magic wrap round the night,
Fleeting yet endless, a shimmering light.

Each heartbeat a treasure, a pulse of the soul,
In this glittering cosmos, we gently lose control.
Dreams woven softly, on a silken thread,
In the quiet allure, let our worries shed.

Time dances slowly in this velvet embrace,
Lost in the glow, every fear we erase.
Captured in starlight, the world fades away,
In this glittering moment, forever we stay.

So breathe in the magic, let the spirit soar,
In the beauty of night, we discover much more.
With hearts intertwined, in a luminous dance,
We find our forever, in this shimmering chance.

Echoes of Bliss

In the soft morning light, the world starts to wake,
Gentle reminders of the paths that we take.
Each moment a note in life's beautiful song,
Echoes of bliss where we all belong.

Footsteps on pathways, a dance in the dew,
Nature sings softly, its praises so true.
With laughter like petals, scattered all near,
In the whispers of joy, our sorrows disappear.

The winds weave their tales through the trees standing
tall,
Inviting our hearts to answer the call.
For every sweet echo is a memory made,
In the symphony of life, where love won't degrade.

So gather the moments, let them fill the air,
In the echoes of bliss, we find love everywhere.
Wrapped in the stories of each passing day,
Together we journey, come what may.

Freedom in the Breeze

The winds whisper soft and low,
Guiding dreams where rivers flow.
With every gust, a spirit roams,
In the air, our heart finds homes.

Through fields where wildflowers dance,
In each breath, we take a chance.
Skyward bound, our souls take flight,
Chasing stars that gleam at night.

Beneath the sun, we freely sway,
Letting go of dull dismay.
In the breeze, we find our way,
And live for now, another day.

In every gust, a sweet release,
In nature's arms, we find our peace.
The freedom sings, a vibrant tune,
Underneath the golden moon.

Elixirs of Laughter

Laughter bubbles, bright and clear,
A sparkling joy that draws us near.
In every chuckle, magic swirls,
We dance through life, adventurous girls.

With friends around, the world's aglow,
In every smile, the love will flow.
Join the chorus of bliss so sweet,
In laughter's arms, we find our feet.

Giggles echo through the night,
Turning shadows into light.
In silly moments, joy is found,
Elixirs of laughter all around.

Moments shared like precious stones,
In the heart, they build their homes.
With each roar and joyous shout,
Elixirs of laughter, there's no doubt.

Kaleidoscope of Hope

In every dream a color shines,
Through every heart, a thread aligns.
A swirl of visions, bright and bold,
In the tapestry, our stories told.

From every crisis, rises light,
In shadows dark, we find our sight.
With open minds, we dare to see,
The world unfolds, a mystery.

Each fragment shines, a truth revealed,
In unity, our fate is sealed.
Together, we can touch the sky,
In the kaleidoscope, dreams never die.

Hope weaves through, a vibrant thread,
In every soul, it gently spreads.
With every twist, new paths we find,
A kaleidoscope of the heart and mind.

Garden of Merriment

In a garden where laughter grows,
Joyful blooms, in sunlight flows.
Each petal soft, a tale to share,
In the air, we feel the care.

The chirping birds in harmony,
Dancing leaves sing symphony.
In every corner, colors gleam,
Filling hearts with light, like a dream.

Among the flowers, friends gather round,
In every smile, happiness found.
With cheerful hearts, we plant the seeds,
In this garden, love us leads.

Through seasons change, the laughter stays,
In memories, we find our ways.
In the garden, forever bright,
Merriment blooms, a pure delight.

Lively Whirlwinds

In the dance of the leaves, they twirl,
Whispers of nature's lively whirl,
A spiraled rush, they spin and play,
Carrying tales of the autumn day.

Bright colors swirl in the golden air,
Each gust a voice, a joyful flair,
With laughter of children, the moment sings,
As the world awakens to what it brings.

Clouds gather as if on cue,
Embracing the shadows, kissed by dew,
A vitality wrapped in tender grace,
In whirlwinds, we find our place.

As the sunset bleeds into night,
Stars emerge with a gentle light,
In lively storms, new dreams begin,
We find our rhythm, we let love in.

Chasing Illumination

In the hush of dawn, I rise,
Chasing light in painted skies,
Each moment glimmers, pure and bright,
An endless dance with morning light.

Waves of gold on the horizon's edge,
Whispers of promise, a sacred pledge,
I seek the glow that fills my heart,
With every step, I'm set apart.

Through shadows deep and valleys low,
I follow beams where soft winds blow,
In flickers found in the darkest night,
I chase the truth, I chase the light.

A lantern's glow in the stillness pure,
Guiding steps with a heart so sure,
In this journey, I seek to find,
The warm embrace of a hopeful mind.

Essence of Bliss

In quiet moments, joy unfolds,
A gentle touch, a story told,
With every breath, the world divine,
Essence of bliss, in hearts entwined.

The rustle of leaves, a soft refrain,
Nature's melody flows through the rain,
Life's simple pleasures, a cherished kiss,
Wrapped in warmth, we find our bliss.

Underneath the starlit skies,
Harmony hums as laughter flies,
In every heartbeat, a magic dance,
In essence of bliss, we take our chance.

With open arms, embrace the day,
Embrace the love that leads the way,
For in this life, we surely see,
The essence of bliss sets our spirits free.

Vibrant Horizons

Beyond the hills where colors blend,
Vibrant horizons, journeys transcend,
A canvas stretched with hues anew,
Ember skies kissed in vibrant blue.

Glowing paths where sunlight spills,
Over the valleys, through the hills,
Each step forward, the world aglow,
In vibrant horizons, our spirits flow.

With each sunrise, a promise clear,
Awakening dreams that draw us near,
The horizon calls, a whispered song,
In its embrace, we all belong.

As twilight beckons, colors fade,
Yet hearts ignited shall never evade,
In vibrant dreams, we find our way,
A journey painted in shades of play.

Joyful Rhapsody

In a meadow where wildflowers bloom,
Laughter echoes, dispelling gloom.
Sunshine dances on dewdrop's face,
Nature's magic leaves a trace.

Birds take flight, their songs so sweet,
With every heartbeat, joy's repeat.
Glimmers of light in every nook,
Life's a story, we've all wrote.

Whispers of wind through trees so tall,
In moments like these, we feel it all.
A rhapsody bursting with colors bright,
Each shared smile, a radiant light.

Together we sing, the world our stage,
Turning the mundane to a joyful page.
In harmony found, hearts start to sway,
This joyful rhapsody guides our way.

Delight in the Ordinary

Morning coffee, steam rises high,
The sun peeks gently, painting the sky.
A quiet moment, just you and me,
Finding beauty in what we see.

A sidewalk cracked, but flowers grow,
In tiny details, love's warmth does flow.
Page of a book turned, stories unfold,
In every mundane, the precious is told.

Footsteps echo on rain-soaked streets,
In every puddle, life just repeats.
A simple smile, a touch of grace,
Delight in the ordinary, we embrace.

Evening shadows stretch far and wide,
In every heartbeat, there's joy inside.
Together we wander, hand in hand,
Finding magic in this simple land.

Serendipity's Embrace

A chance meeting on a crowded street,
Unexpected laughter, strangers greet.
In moments fleeting, silence ends,
The universe smiles, calling friends.

Whispers of fate in every glance,
Life unfolds with a perfect dance.
Coincidences weave a curious thread,
Through tangled paths, where hearts are led.

Stars align in the moonlit night,
Guiding lost souls towards the light.
In serendipity, the heart can race,
Wrapped in the warmth of love's embrace.

Tomorrow may hold what we can't foresee,
In every heartbeat, joy's decree.
With open arms, we dare to chance,
For serendipity blooms in every glance.

The Tapestry of Light

Threads of silver, strands of gold,
Stories of lives, both brave and bold.
Woven together, a vivid display,
The tapestry of light shows the way.

Moments of joy are stitched with care,
Each one a memory, vibrant and fair.
Through laughter and sorrow, we find our place,
In the intricate web, we embrace grace.

Colors of sunset, hues that blend,
A beautiful canvas where dreams transcend.
In shadows cast, brilliant sparks ignite,
Creating the masterpiece, pure delight.

In every heart, a unique hue,
A tapestry crafted, both old and new.
Together we shine, our spirits ignite,
In the warm embrace of this tapestry of light.

The Magic of Togetherness

In laughter's embrace, we find our way,
With hands intertwined, we greet the day.
Through shadows and light, we share our dreams,
In the dance of our hearts, nothing's as it seems.

Like stars that shine in the velvet night,
Together we spark, our spirits alight.
Each moment a treasure, woven with care,
In the tapestry of life, forever we share.

With whispers of joy, our souls take flight,
In the warmth of your smile, all fears take flight.
Through trials we face, we rise and stand tall,
In the magic of togetherness, we conquer all.

As seasons change, our bond remains strong,
In the symphony of love, we both belong.
Hand in hand, we journey through time,
In the magic of togetherness, we forever rhyme.

Unraveled Happiness

In the morning light, smiles bloom anew,
Moments of joy in the simple and true.
We chase the sun, our hearts full of glee,
In the dance of today, we just let it be.

With laughter that echoes, we chase each whim,
In the river of dreams, we joyfully swim.
Unraveled happiness, like flowers in spring,
In each little thing, our spirits take wing.

Through valleys of doubt, we find our way,
In the warmth of your hand, I'm never led astray.
With each shared glance, a spark ignites,
In the journey of love, we reach new heights.

As shadows dance softly, we sing our song,
In the heart of the moment, we both belong.
Unraveled happiness, forever in sight,
In the glow of our bond, the world feels right.

The Essence of Glee

In morning light, a smile shines bright,
Joy dances lightly, heart takes flight.
Laughter echoes through the air,
Sweet melodies, nothing compares.

With every step, the world feels new,
Colors vibrant, in every hue.
A carefree spirit, shining bold,
Moments cherished, stories told.

In the gentle breeze, hope does sway,
Chasing shadows, fears kept at bay.
Hands held tight, we share the bliss,
In simple things, we find our kiss.

Whispers of joy, pure and free,
Life's great treasure, the essence of glee.
Together we wander, hearts ablaze,
In laughter and love, we spend our days.

Celestial Playfulness

Stars twinkle gently, a cosmic dance,
Moonbeams waltz in a trance.
Galaxies spin, a radiant show,
Through night's embrace, whimsically flow.

Clouds drift softly, with dreams they play,
In the vast sky, they frolic and sway.
Laughter echoes in the pale moonlight,
Whims of the cosmos, a delightful sight.

Planets giggle, in silent delight,
As comets dash in a joyful flight.
The universe hums a playful tune,
Celebrating joy under the moon.

In the starry expanse, we find our grace,
Celestial joy, our hearts embrace.
Together we soar on stardust wings,
In the heart of the night, pure bliss it brings.

Jubilee of the Soul

In every heartbeat, a rhythm sings,
Life bursts forth, its joy it brings.
A jubilee, vibrant and bright,
Awakening hearts to love's pure light.

Through valleys deep, and mountains high,
The spirit dances, reaching the sky.
Each step a blessing, each breath a song,
In this celebration, we all belong.

Memories woven, a tapestry grand,
Connected we stand, hand in hand.
With open hearts, we share the grace,
In the jubilee, find our place.

Lifted by laughter, cradled in peace,
In this joy, all troubles cease.
A dance of souls under sunlit roles,
In the jubilee, we areWhole, we are whole.

Waves of Euphoria

The ocean roars, a vibrant heart,
With every wave, a fresh new start.
In foam and spray, pure joy cascades,
A symphony of life, never fades.

Under the sun, we bask and play,
The tide of happiness guides our way.
Footprints trailing in golden sand,
Together we laugh, hand in hand.

As the sun dips low, the colors blend,
In this moment, our spirits mend.
Each crashing wave, a message sent,
Euphoria flows, time is spent.

In depths of blue, our dreams take flight,
Riding the waves of pure delight.
With hearts wide open, we dive into,
Waves of euphoria, always anew.

Revelry in Simplicity

In quiet corners, laughter flows,
A gentle breeze where sunlight glows.
Barefoot wanderers, hearts so light,
Chasing shadows from day to night.

Crickets sing their evening song,
Under the stars where we belong.
With every sip of nature's brew,
Joy is painted in every hue.

Each simple moment, pure delight,
A dance of fireflies in the night.
We savor time with every breath,
In simple pleasure, find our depth.

Surrounded by the things we love,
As earth whispers secrets from above.
In revelry, our spirits soar,
In simplicity, we ask for more.

Ultimate Playfulness

Bubbles floating in the air,
Children giggle, without a care.
Rainbow colors dance around,
In this joy, we are unbound.

Laughter echoes, games arise,
Chasing dreams beneath the skies.
Hopscotch lines and silly grins,
In every loss, a world of wins.

From swings that soar to slides that thrill,
The heart races, our spirits fill.
With every twist, with every spin,
Ultimate playfulness begins.

Imagination leads the way,
In a world where we can play.
Lost in wonder, time stands still,
In this moment, hearts we fill.

Magic in the Mundane

Morning dew on blades of grass,
In the stillness, moments pass.
A teacup warms in tender hands,
Quiet magic in everyday lands.

The hum of life, a gentle sound,
In the ordinary, joy is found.
Familiar paths and faces greet,
Each moment bittersweet, complete.

Sunset paints the sky with gold,
In soft rays, our stories told.
Little wonders, soft and sweet,
In the mundane, our hearts meet.

With every breath, we recognize,
Magic lives within our eyes.
In every task, a touch of grace,
In the mundane, we find our place.

Glowing Connections

In twilight's glow, two hearts converse,
Words like whispers, subtle and terse.
Shared moments weave an unseen thread,
In each heartbeat, love is fed.

With laughter bright as stars at night,
We find our way, our souls take flight.
In glances shared, our dreams align,
In glowing connections, love will shine.

Through gentle words and tender grace,
We etch the paths we long to trace.
Together, hand in hand, we stand,
In every touch, the world expands.

Every silence, every sigh,
Holds the promise of the sky.
In glowing warmth, we learn to see,
The threads of love that bind you and me.

Serendipity's Embrace

In twilight's glow, we find our way,
Accidental paths weave night and day.
Whispers of fate, soft as a breeze,
Leading our hearts, putting them at ease.

Moments collide, a chance so rare,
In the simplest things, love fills the air.
Laughter dances, tides of delight,
Serendipity's glow, our guiding light.

With every turn, the unknown awaits,
Opening doors to our shared fates.
Hand in hand, we wander free,
Entwined by the magic of mystery.

In starlit nights, our spirits soar,
With every heartbeat, we crave for more.
In serendipity, our souls align,
A journey of wonder, forever divine.

Euphoria's Dance

Under the moonlight, we twirl and spin,
In euphoria's grasp, our joy begins.
Laughter erupts like fireworks bright,
A symphony played in the still of night.

Colors burst forth, emotions ignited,
Every heartbeat, vividly invited.
A melody sweet, carrying us high,
Floating on dreams, like clouds in the sky.

Hands intertwine, bodies entranced,
Lost in the rhythm of this bold dance.
Every twirl whispered promises new,
In euphoria's spell, just me and you.

Beneath the stars, with spirits uncaged,
We chase the moments, joyfully engaged.
In this embrace, our hearts take flight,
Euphoria's dance, a love-soaked night.

Shimmering Dreams

In a realm where stars collide,
Shimmering dreams, our hearts confide.
Whispers of hope in the night sky,
A world without limits, where wishes fly.

Waves of silver, glistening bright,
Carry our thoughts in the quiet night.
With every heartbeat, visions take form,
A tapestry woven, our hopes keep warm.

In gentle moments, reflections gleam,
Caught in the magic of our shared dream.
With eyes wide open, we harness the light,
Shimmering dreams, guiding us right.

As dawn approaches, visions transform,
Bringing our dreams into radiant form.
With courage we step into the day,
Shimmering dreams, lighting the way.

The Art of Smiles

A smile exchanged, soft as the dawn,
Crafting connections that carry us on.
In fleeting moments, warmth is found,
The art of smiles, love unbound.

With every curve, a story unfolds,
In the language of joy, the heart beholds.
A simple gesture, a gentle embrace,
The art of smiles, our timeless grace.

Through laughter shared and tears set free,
Smiles build bridges between you and me.
A glance that lingers, a spark ignites,
In life's vast canvas, love paints the nights.

So let us share this precious gift,
With every smile, our spirits lift.
In the tapestry of life, we find style,
In the gentle art, the art of smiles.

The Warmth of Togetherness

In quiet moments shared at dusk,
Hearts entwined in gentle trust.
Laughter echoes in the air,
Togetherness beyond compare.

Hand in hand, we face the night,
With every step, our spirits bright.
The world outside may fade away,
But here with you, I long to stay.

In every smile, a story's told,
A tapestry of warmth to hold.
Through trials faced, we stand as one,
A bond unbroken, never done.

As seasons change, our love will grow,
Like rivers flowing, ever slow.
In this embrace, we find our place,
Together always, a warm embrace.

Unconstrained Elation

With arms wide open, hearts in flight,
We dance beneath the stars so bright.
Joy spills over, wild and free,
In each small moment, pure glee.

The world a canvas, bold and new,
Every shade an endless hue.
Laughter rings through fields of gold,
A treasure trove of dreams to hold.

Spinning round in endless delight,
Chasing shadows into the night.
Each heartbeat sings a vibrant song,
In this embrace, we all belong.

Let worries fade, let spirits soar,
In the magic of now, we explore.
Unconstrained, we rise and play,
In the joy of this bright day.

New Dawn's Promise

The dawn breaks soft, a gentle light,
Whispers of hope in the quiet night.
Each ray a promise, fresh and clear,
A chance to grow, to shed our fear.

With every hue, the day awakes,
A world reborn, a path it makes.
The sky, a palette, rich and vast,
Reminds us of moments gone, hold fast.

Dreams take flight with morning's kiss,
In the stillness, find our bliss.
The future waits with arms so wide,
Embrace the journey, let love guide.

New beginnings call our name,
In the sunrise, stoke the flame.
Together we will rise and shine,
In this journey, your hand in mine.

Tidal Waves of Cheer

Like waves that crash upon the shore,
Laughter spills, and spirits soar.
In rhythmic dance, our joys collide,
A joyful tide, let us abide.

With every crest, a moment shared,
In tender hearts, we've boldly dared.
The ocean's song, a sweet refrain,
In waves of cheer, we feel no pain.

Amidst the foam, we find our way,
In each embrace, come what may.
Together, we shall ride the swell,
In joyous notes, a tale to tell.

So here we stand, forever true,
In tidal waves, just me and you.
Let laughter echo, wide and free,
In this vast sea, our hearts will be.

Threads of Delight

In the garden of dreams, we play,
Woven colors dance in the day.
Each thread spun with care and grace,
Brightened hearts in this sacred space.

Whispers of joy in the light,
Stitching memories, oh so bright.
With every laugh, every sigh,
We weave a tapestry, you and I.

Moments glimmer, soft and sweet,
Entwined footsteps, a rhythmic beat.
In silent harmony, we grow,
Threads of delight in the flow.

Embracing life, hand in hand,
Building dreams upon the sand.
With every stitch, a story told,
Threads of delight, a treasure to hold.

Illuminated Moments

In twilight's glow, shadows play,
Stars awaken, mark the way.
Each flicker tells a tale anew,
Illuminated moments, bright and true.

Laughter dances in the air,
A tapestry of hope laid bare.
Time slips softly, whispers near,
Sparkling memories, crystal clear.

Through the lens of now, we see,
Fleeting seconds, wild and free.
Joy reflected in each glance,
Illuminated moments, a sweet dance.

As dusk serenades the night,
Hearts ignited, pure and bright.
In every pause, a glow remains,
Illuminated moments, love's refrains.

Heartfelt Echoes

In quiet corners, whispers rise,
Heartfelt echoes, love's soft guise.
With every beat, a story shared,
In timeless rhythms, we've all bared.

Beneath the stars, we unite,
A symphony of warmth, pure light.
Each echo holds a memory dear,
Entwined laughter, and joyful cheer.

Through trials faced, we band together,
Heartfelt echoes in all weather.
Every challenge, hand in hand,
Building bridges, a loving strand.

As seasons change, our voices blend,
Heartfelt echoes that never end.
In harmony, we find our way,
Together forever, come what may.

The Essence of Laughter

In gentle breezes, laughter flies,
The essence golden, softly sighs.
Each chuckle weaves a vibrant thread,
Through moments shared and words unsaid.

A spark ignites within our hearts,
The essence of laughter, life imparts.
With every giggle, joy ignites,
Casting shadows into the lights.

In playful banter, spirits soar,
The essence of laughter, we adore.
Bringing warmth to the coldest day,
In each shared smile, we find our way.

Through trials faced and paths unclear,
Laughter echoes, casting out fear.
In each embrace, we find our bliss,
The essence of laughter, love's gentle kiss.

9 789916 882115